Next Generation **ENERGY**

ENERGY FROM WATER

Hydroelectric, Tidal, and Wave Power

Nancy Dickmann

CRABTREE
Publishing Company
www.crabtreebooks.com

Crabtree Publishing Company

www.crabtreebooks.com

Author: Nancy Dickmann

Editors: Sarah Eason and Jennifer Sanderson
and Petrice Custance

Proofreader: Katie Dicker

Editorial director: Kathy Middleton

Design: Paul Myerscough and Jessica Moon

Cover design: Paul Myerscough

Photo research: Sarah Eason and Jennifer Sanderson

Prepress technician: Tammy McGarr

Print coordinator: Margaret Amy Salter

Consultant: Richard Spilsbury, degree in Zoology,
author and editor of educational science books
for 30 years

Production coordinated by Calcium Creative

Photo Credits:

t=Top, bl=Bottom Left, br=Bottom Right

Dreamstime: Airphoto: p. 18; Harold W Bradley: pp. 18–19; James
Wheeler: p. 19; Jaroslav Frank: pp. 16–17; Jinyoung Lee: pp. 20–21, 30–31;
Wisconsinart: p. 16; Shutterstock: p. 28; EpicStockMedia: p. 4; Adwo:
pp. 22–23; Alex Mit: pp. 3, 26–27; Alexandr Vlassyuk: pp. 6–7, 32; Beer
Worawut: pp. 4–5, 28–29; Bonita R. Cheshier: pp. 10–11; Craig Hanson:
p. 27; Farbled: p. 17; Jejim: p. 7; Juergen Faelchle: p. 8; Kucher Serhii: pp.
14–15; Kunal Mehta: p. 10; Kustov: p. 9; Matyas Rehak: p. 13; Pedrosala:
pp. 8–9; PhotonCatcher: p. 6; Randy Andy: pp. 24–25; Rita Robinson: p.
12; Snapgalleria: p. 11; Snvv: p. 24; Stefano Ember: pp. 12–13; Suzanne
Tucker: p. 23; Tracing Tea: p. 14; Tupungato: p. 1; V. J. Matthew: p. 25;
Vilainecrevette p. 22; Wikimedia Commons: Mindlessworker: p. 26;
P123: p. 21; User:Vmenkov: p. 15; U.S. Federal Government/Lance Cpl.
Vanessa M. American Horse: pp. 3 br, 20.

Cover, p. 1: Shutterstock: Tupungato.

Cover and title page image: The hydroelectric power station at Hoover
Dam on the border of Arizona and Nevada, USA

Library and Archives Canada Cataloguing in Publication

Dickmann, Nancy, author
        Energy from water : hydroelectric, tidal, and wave power /
Nancy Dickmann.

(Next generation energy)
Includes index.
Issued in print and electronic formats.
ISBN 978-0-7787-2380-6 (bound).--
ISBN 978-0-7787-2384-4 (paperback).--
ISBN 978-1-4271-1757-1 (html)

        1. Water-power--Juvenile literature. 2. Tidal power--Juvenile
literature. 3. Renewable energy sources--Juvenile literature. 4.
Hydroelectric power plants--Juvenile literature. I. Title.

TC146.D53 2016   j333.91′4   C2015-907825-3
                                        C2015-907826-1

Library of Congress Cataloging-in-Publication Data

Names: Dickmann, Nancy, author.
Title: Energy from water : hydroelectric, tidal, and wave power /
    Nancy Dickmann.
Description: Crabtree Publishing Company, [2016] | Series:
    Next generation energy | Includes index. | Description based
    on print version record and CIP data provided by publisher;
    resource not viewed.
Identifiers: LCCN 2015045109 (print) | LCCN 2015044045 (ebook)
    | ISBN 9781427117571 (electronic HTML) | ISBN 9780778723806
    (reinforced library binding : alk. paper) | ISBN 9780778723844
    (pbk. : alk. paper)
Subjects: LCSH: Water-power--Juvenile literature. | Tidal power-
    -Juvenile literature. | Renewable energy sources--Juvenile
    literature. | Hydroelectric power plants--Juvenile literature.
Classification: LCC TC146 (print) | LCC TC146 .D53 2016 (ebook)
    | DDC 333.91/4--dc23
LC record available at http://lccn.loc.gov/2015045109

Crabtree Publishing Company

www.crabtreebooks.com   1-800-387-7650

Printed in Canada/012016/BF20151123

Published in Canada
Crabtree Publishing
616 Welland Ave.
St. Catharines, Ontario
L2M 5V6

Published in the United States
Crabtree Publishing
PMB 59051
350 Fifth Avenue, 59th Floor
New York, New York 10118

Published in the United Kingdom
Crabtree Publishing
Maritime House
Basin Road North, Hove
BN41 1WR

Published in Australia
Crabtree Publishing
3 Charles Street
Coburg North
VIC, 3058

Contents

Types of Energy   4

Moving Water   6

Renewable Energy   8

How a Dam Works   10

Where in the World?   12

Small Solutions   14

Environmental Impact   16

Benefits of Hydroelectricity   18

Wave Power   20

Waves: For and Against   22

Tidal Power   24

Tidal Pros and Cons   26

Power Up!   28

Glossary   30

Learning More   31

Index   32

Types of Energy

A skier stands at the top of a mountain, ready to begin the descent. Being at the top of a steep slope gives her potential **energy,** which is the energy an object has because of its position, not its motion. Once she uses her muscles to push off, Earth's **gravity** will pull her down the slope. Her potential energy turns into kinetic energy, or energy from movement.

We use energy all the time in our daily lives. Some of the energy we use harnesses the power of kinetic energy. Blowing wind and flowing water are forms of kinetic energy that can be converted into electrical energy. This electricity can then be used for many different things, from charging a cell phone to powering a car. We get our energy from other sources, too. We burn **fuels**, such as coal or oil. We generate heat energy from **chemical reactions**. We use panels to collect energy from sunlight.

Hydroelectric power, which is electricity generated from moving water, is one of the cleanest energy sources in use. However, no energy source is perfect: some create pollution, some are too expensive, and some contribute to the warming of Earth and global **climate change**.

This surfer depends on the kinetic energy of the wind to push the ocean's water into waves.

Using Energy

Earth's energy needs are increasing all the time. The planet's population is increasing, and each person uses more energy than they did a few decades ago. Lifestyles have changed. We have become used to traveling by car or airplane, and depend on appliances and gadgets that make our daily lives easier. These all require power in some form. How can we continue to meet all of our energy demands? Our challenge for the future is to find clean, low-cost sources of energy that are **sustainable**. This means living in a way that conserves and efficiently uses natural resources.

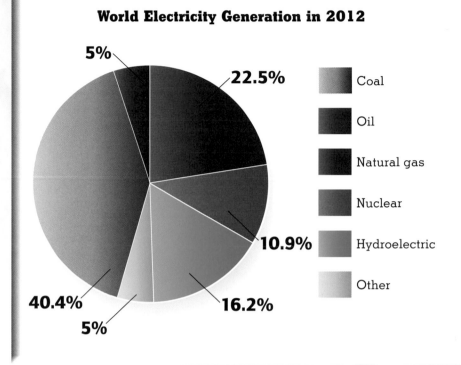

World Electricity Generation in 2012

- 5%
- 22.5%
- 10.9%
- 16.2%
- 5%
- 40.4%

Legend:
- Coal
- Oil
- Natural gas
- Nuclear
- Hydroelectric
- Other

Hydroelectric power already makes up a significant percentage of the world's electricity supply.

REWIND

For hundreds of years, people have used the energy of the wind, Sun, and water in various forms. For example, the wind can fill the sails of a ship and push it forward, or turn the blades of a windmill that grinds grain. Today, we harness their power to generate electricity. Electricity lights our homes and powers our devices. Do you think this is a better use of these natural forms of energy? Give reasons for your answer.

Moving Water

The water on Earth's surface is rarely still. Rivers flow from high ground to lower ground, and wind pushes water into currents and waves that sweep across the world's oceans. Rain falls from the sky to the ground. All this shows that water has a lot of kinetic energy.

Thousands of years ago, the ancient Greeks harnessed the power of moving water to turn waterwheels. People also used moving water for transportation, sending ships and barges loaded with goods from city to city on rivers. This allowed them to transport loads that would be too heavy for horses or oxen to pull.

In the early 1800s, **engineers** worked on ways to make waterwheels more efficient. They could use waterwheels to power machines, such as weaving looms, in factories. The first use of moving water to generate electricity was in a house called Cragside, in northern England. The house's owner developed his own hydroelectric factory that powered electric lighting. The first **commercial** hydroelectric factory opened in Wisconsin in 1882, but it produced only a small amount of electricity.

Long ago, waterwheels were often used to turn the heavy stones that ground grain into flour.

Hydropower Today

The Wisconsin plant was the start of a type of new hydroelectric project. Hydroelectricity makes up 7 percent of the electricity in the United States today. In other countries the percentage is much higher. For example, Canada is the second-largest producer of hydroelectricity after China. Hydroelectricity makes up about 59 percent of Canada's electricity supply. Most of this electricity comes from power plants built on rivers, but we are starting to use the power of waves and **tides**, too. However, although hydropower can be used to charge electric vehicles, it cannot directly replace oil and natural gas for fueling engines.

The construction of the Three Gorges Hydroelectric Dam in China is still controversial. After it was built, huge areas of land were flooded on purpose, forcing more than 1 million people to move from their homes and farms.

REWIND

When the Fox River hydroelectric plant in Wisconsin was built, it generated only enough electricity to light the plant itself and two other buildings. Today, the world's largest hydroelectric plant, China's Three Gorges Dam, generates huge amounts of electricity—roughly equivalent to burning 49 million tons (44.5 million metric tons) of coal. Do you think hydropower can become even more efficient? Explain your answer.

Renewable Energy

There are many different words used to describe energy sources: clean, green, renewable, and sustainable, to name a few. It can be confusing, but most of these words refer to one of two things: an energy source's impact on the environment, or whether it is likely to ever run out.

Some energy sources cause problems for the planet. For example, burning **fossil fuels**, such as oil or coal, releases **carbon dioxide**. When this gas collects in the atmosphere, it helps trap the Sun's heat, which warms the planet. This temperature increase contributes to global climate change, which is causing polar ice to melt faster and causing extreme forms of weather. Some fuels pollute the air or water, which can harm plants and animals as well as damage human health. Even energy sources that are considered clean can cause environmental damage. For example, building a **dam** for a hydroelectric plant can flood farmland and destroy **habitats**.

Solar power is a renewable source of energy. However, electricity can be generated by solar power only when the Sun shines. Some places do not get enough sunshine for it to be effective.

An Endless Supply?

Fossil fuels such as coal, oil, and gas were formed millions of years ago. At some point in the next century or two, we will have used up Earth's supply of these fuels. Fossil fuels are called nonrenewable because the supply cannot be replaced. **Nuclear power** is also nonrenewable because the uranium that fuels nuclear power stations will eventually run out. On the other hand, the Sun will keep shining for billions of years, and winds will keep blowing. We will never run out of solar or wind power, so these energy sources are called renewable.

Although we still depend on fossil fuels for a large percentage of our energy needs, renewable sources are slowly catching up. Most experts agree that shifting to renewable energy will help protect the planet and ensure that we have access to energy far into the future.

Mining a fossil fuel, such as coal, is dirty and polluting. So is burning it for energy.

The Energy Future: You Choose

Electricity from renewable sources is often more expensive than electricity produced by burning fossil fuels. Solar and wind farms and hydroelectric plants are expensive to build. However, once they are built, they are fairly cheap to run. Improved technology should also help costs come down. Do you think it is worth paying more now for renewable electricity? Why or why not?

How a Dam Works

Hydroelectric plants are usually located on rivers, and many involve building a dam to create a reservoir to hold the water. The power is generated from falling water, so the best spot for a dam is where the river has a large drop in elevation, or height. The amount of electricity a hydroelectric plant can produce depends on the amount of water and how far it falls.

When a dam is built across a river, it stops the flow of water along the river's course. Water builds up behind the dam, forming a reservoir. As the reservoir grows, the water builds up potential energy. A dam has gates that can be opened and closed to control the amount of water flowing through.

When the gates are opened, water rushes through and travels downward through a pipe called a **penstock**. The penstock carries the water to the **turbines**. These devices have hundreds of blades, and when the water rushes over the blades, it makes the turbines spin. This rotation spins powerful magnets that generate an electric current. The electricity produced is then sent out through wires to wherever it is needed.

Lake Mead in Nevada is actually a reservoir created by the construction of the Hoover Dam.

Run of the River

Hydroelectric plants that do not use dams are called run-of-the-river plants. They usually produce less electricity than big dams. To work effectively, they must be built on rivers with a steady, natural flow. A low wall, called a **weir**, is built across the river to change the direction of its flow into a penstock. The force of gravity pulls the water downward as it spins the turbines. Then, the water is redirected back to the natural flow of the river. Run-of-the-river plants may generate less electricity than large dams, but they usually cause less disruption to the surrounding area.

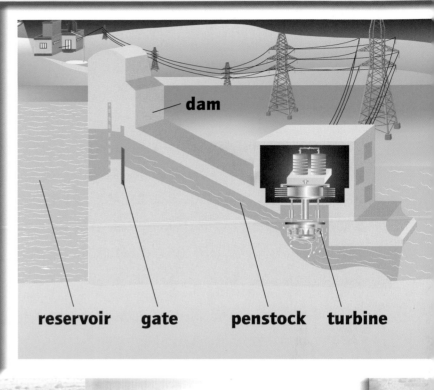

dam

reservoir   gate   penstock   turbine

This diagram shows the main parts of a hydroelectric dam.

FAST FORWARD

Hydroelectric power is dependent on a consistent supply of running water. **Droughts** and water shortages can affect the amount of hydroelectricity that can be generated. For example, in 2012, California had a 38 percent drop in hydroelectric energy production as a result of water shortages. Water is a precious resource that must be conserved. If we keep wasting water, what might happen in the future? How will this affect hydroelectric power? Give reasons for your answers.

Where in the World?

Hydroelectricity is the most widely used renewable source of electricity around the world, with more than 150 countries generating at least some electricity this way. There are hundreds of dams around the world, with more being planned and built. Millions of people use hydropower to meet their electricity needs.

The building of the Three Gorges Dam helped China become the biggest producer of hydroelectricity in the world. However, hydroelectricity makes up less than 20 percent of China's total production of electricity. Brazil's hydroelectric output is lower than China's, but it makes up about 80 percent of the country's total electricity production.

Canada, the United States, Norway, and Russia are also big producers of hydroelectricity. Many smaller countries produce a lot less, but it makes up a much larger percentage of their total electricity usage. Countries such as Albania, Ethiopia, Mozambique, Nepal, and Paraguay generate 100 percent of their electricity from hydropower. This means that they do not need to burn fossil fuels in power plants.

The Chief Joseph Dam is a run-of-the-river hydroelectric power station located on the Columbia River, in Washington State.

Where Next?

Hydroelectric plants cannot be built just anywhere. For example, very flat areas are unsuitable. A large hydroelectric plant requires a big river and a good drop in elevation. In some of the more developed countries, such as the United States, many of the best sites are already being used. However, there are still opportunities for new dams in many locations around the world, particularly in South America, Central Africa, India, and China. In some poorer areas, the development of hydroelectric power is slow because dams can be so expensive to build.

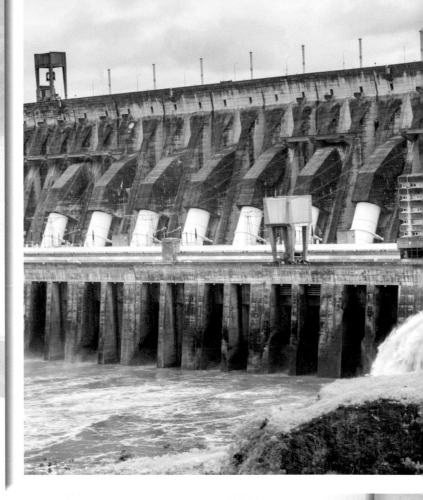

The Itaipu Dam in South America is the second-largest hydroelectric facility in the world. It provides about 17 percent of the electricity used in Brazil, and 75 percent of Paraguay's supply.

REWIND

The Itaipu Dam was built in the 1970s. It lies on the Paraná River, which forms the border between Brazil and Paraguay. The river also flows into Argentina. Argentina's government was worried that if Brazil opened the floodgates, it could flood their capital city, Buenos Aires. So before construction began, Argentina, Brazil, and Paraguay signed an agreement about water levels in the river. Do you think the need for an international agreement might sometimes make new hydroelectric projects more complicated? Explain your answer.

Small Solutions

The biggest hydroelectric installations provide power for hundreds of thousands, or even millions, of people. However, hydroelectricity does not have to be big to be effective. Suitable locations for giant dams are limited, but there are many that are perfect for small-scale hydroelectricity projects.

The potential energy output of a hydroelectric power plant is usually measured in **megawatts** (MW). Many large plants have a capacity of 2,000 to 5,000 MW, and a few giant dams can produce even more. At the other end of the scale, small-scale hydropower plants have an installation with a capacity of just 1 to 20 MW.

The smallest hydropower projects have a capacity of fewer than 1 MW, and can power a single home or provide limited electricity for a small community. They are especially useful in poor rural areas, where they may be the only source of electricity.

This small-scale hydro project has gates that can be opened and closed to control the flow of water.

How Do They Work?

Small-scale hydro projects can work on smaller rivers and streams. They need either a reasonable amount of water flowing along, or a fairly large drop in elevation—or ideally, both. The project will be most effective if the river's flow is fairly constant throughout the year.

Most projects are run-of-the-river, so they do not involve building a dam or creating a reservoir. Some use existing structures, such as a weir. This makes them more affordable to set up. Part of the river's flow is diverted into a place called an **intake**. From there it is taken to the penstock, which is the pipe that takes the water to the turbine. After spinning the turbine, the water is channeled back to the river.

This small-scale hydro plant in Hongping, China, harnesses the kinetic energy of water coming down a mountain through a pipe.

FAST FORWARD

Small-scale hydropower can make a real difference to small or isolated communities in poorer countries. For example, the Bungin Micro Hydro Project in Indonesia has a capacity of 85 to 90 **kilowatts** (kW) of electricity, which is sold to 265 homes. Some of the profit is used to help local businesses or provide scholarships. Could projects like these help meet the growing energy needs of the developing world? Explain your answer.

Environmental Impact

Even though hydroelectricity is a very clean energy source, it does have some disadvantages. It can be used only in locations near water and the costs of building a large dam can be huge. Another problem is that drought can sometimes affect the amount of electricity that a dam can produce. Hydroelectricity projects can also have a negative impact on the environment.

Building a dam and a reservoir can mean flooding large areas of land. The reservoir created by the Itaipu Dam covers 520 square miles (1,350 sq km). Although that is smaller than the state of Rhode Island, nearly 60,000 people living on the land were forced to leave their homes when the waters rose. As they flow, rivers carry tiny particles of rock, earth, and plant material, called sediment. A dam disrupts the flow of sediment in a river. Sediment builds up in the reservoir. This can lead to the erosion of **deltas** and other shore features.

When the Aswan Dam was built on the Nile River in the 1960s, this ancient Egyptian temple had to be relocated. It was moved, stone by stone, to higher ground so it would not be under water.

The Environment at Risk

When land is flooded to create a reservoir, it does not just destroy human settlements. It also destroys habitats, pushing animals into other areas. A dam also creates a barrier in the river, causing problems for animals, such as salmon and trout, which need to move up and downstream as part of their life cycles.

In a reservoir, the trees and other plants submerged under the water start to rot. This creates methane, which is released into the atmosphere when the water moves through the turbines. Methane is a **greenhouse gas**, with an even stronger warming effect than carbon dioxide. More study is needed, but it is possible that some reservoirs could have just as much impact on climate change as a coal-fired power plant.

A fish ladder is a series of pools that allows fish to jump over a dam, one step at a time. This helps them travel upstream to breed.

REWIND

Huge storms and earthquakes can destroy dams. In 1975, a large storm made the water level of the Ru River in China rise. The rising river broke through the Banqiao Dam, sending the equivalent of 280,000 Olympic-sized swimming pools of water flooding down into the valley below. Whole towns were destroyed and 171,000 people died. Could a similar disaster happen again? Explain your answer.

Benefits of Hydroelectricity

Switching from fossil fuels to more renewable types of energy is one of the biggest challenges facing the world today. Fossil fuels are cheap and easy to use, while renewable energy is often more expensive to generate or is unavailable in some areas. However, the potential benefits of hydroelectricity make it one of the most attractive renewable energy sources.

Hydroelectricity could be the key to reducing dependence on power plants fueled by coal, oil, or natural gas.

Sustainability: Hydroelectricity is renewable, as rainfall renews the water in rivers and reservoirs.

Cost: Large dams and power plants can be expensive to build. However, once they are in place, the cost to operate a hydroelectric plant is fairly low because the water is free. Small-scale hydro projects are much cheaper to build. They are often very cost-effective.

Consistency: Unlike solar or wind power, which generate electricity only when the Sun shines or the wind blows, hydroelectric power provides a consistent supply of energy.

Flexibility: The operators of a hydroelectric plant can adjust the amount of water flowing through it. When power consumption, or usage, is low, water is simply stored in the reservoir to be used later when demand is high.

Pollution: No fuel is burned in a hydroelectric plant, so there is minimal air and water pollution. The power plant itself does not release greenhouse gases. The release of methane from some reservoirs is a problem, but we need more research to understand its effects.

Ease of use: The technology for generating hydroelectric power, from tiny projects to massive dams, is tried and tested.

Safety: Compared to some other sources of energy, such as nuclear power and fossil fuels, hydroelectric power is much safer to produce.

Canada is a big producer of renewable energy. Less than 20 percent of its electricity is generated by burning fossil fuels.

The Energy Future: You Choose

Like all types of energy, hydroelectric power has its advantages and disadvantages. Large dams produce a lot of power, but they often have a massive impact on the surrounding area. Small-scale hydro projects are less disruptive, but they can supply only a limited amount of electricity. Would you support a proposal for a small-scale hydroelectric project in your local area? How would you feel if the building of a large dam meant that your family had to move to a new area? Give reasons to support your answers.

19

Wave Power

Rivers are not the only places where we can generate electricity from the energy of moving water. Ocean waves contain a lot of kinetic energy. The movement of warm and cool air causes wind to push ocean water into waves. Until fairly recently, we did not have an effective way of harnessing this energy. We now have a variety of ways to harness the energy and below are a few examples.

One method of generating electricity from waves is with an oscillating water column. A chamber is built on the shore. When waves arrive, they make the water level inside the chamber rise and fall, forcing air in and out of a hole at the top of the chamber. As the air moves, it spins a turbine.

Other wave energy converters (WECs) float on top of the water. One of the first to be built was the Pelamis WEC in 1999. This is a floating tube about the length of five train cars. It has hinged joints and as it bobs up and down in the waves, the hinges bend. When they bend, they pump high-pressure oil and this powers the electrical **generators**.

Some WECs do not float on the surface. For example, the CETO technology is located completely underwater. **Buoys** are placed a few feet below the surface, and they are tethered, or tied, to pumps that are moored to the seabed. The buoys move up and down with the motion of passing waves, which drives the pumps. They pump pressurized water through a pipeline to the shore, and this drives a turbine.

This wave power buoy, located off the coast of Oahu, Hawaii, can provide electricity for two homes.

Wave Farms

A wave farm is a collection of machines in the same location that generate electricity from the power of waves. Wave farms are in development in a few places. So far, wave energy generates only a tiny percentage of the world's electricity. As technology improves, wave farms may become more common.

The world's first commercial wave farm, in Portugal, used Pelamis devices like this one (right).

REWIND

The first commercial wave farm was opened in Portugal in 2008. It used three Pelamis WECs and was designed to provide electricity for up to 1,500 homes. However, the machines developed a fault and before they could be fixed, the company that ran the wave farm went out of business. A few years later, the Pelamis company went out of business, too. Wave power technology still needs a lot of **investment**— money that many countries do not have. Give reasons to persuade governments and businesses to invest in wave power technology.

Waves: For and Against

Although wave power has the potential to provide huge amounts of electricity, it has been used only in a few places so far. The technology is fairly new and engineers are still working on ways to make it more efficient. One day, it may be able to compete with more established sources of power.

There are several advantages to using wave power. Using waves to generate electricity does not use up water or other natural resources. Wave power is renewable because the oceans' waves will always be there. The waves move constantly all day and all night, so wave turbines can provide a consistent source of power.

Once the machines are up and running, wave power is pollution-free and does not release greenhouse gases. Wave farms can be built out at sea, which reduces some of their environmental impacts. Wave power is very efficient: a wave farm covering fewer than 0.5 square miles (1.3 sq km) has the potential to power several thousand homes.

A big disadvantage of installing wave power machinery on the ocean floor is that it can disturb the habitats of animals such as sea stars.

Wave Power Problems

At the moment, one of the main problems with wave power is the cost. It is very expensive to set up a wave farm, and it may be years before this investment is earned back. The machines can also be damaged by storms and constant exposure to salt water. The need to maintain and replace the equipment can lead to higher costs.

Wave power also has an environmental impact. There are studies being done to see how wave machines affect ocean habitats and wildlife. Wave farms on the shore could also interfere with leisure activities for local residents or tourism. Many coasts are also protected areas, which means wave farms would not be allowed there.

Many people do not want to see or hear a wave energy generator when they go to the beach.

The Energy Future: You Choose

To be most useful, a wave farm has to be located fairly close to a city or populated area. However, the coast near a city is often a busy place. Cargo ships, cruise ships, and private boats may all use the harbor. Local residents and tourists want an attractive, unspoiled beach. The coastal landscape and wildlife need to be protected, too. If you were the mayor of a coastal city, would you support a wave farm in the area? How would you balance the needs of everyone in the city? Give reasons for your answers.

Tidal Power

About every 12 hours, the oceans rise and fall with the tides. Tides are caused by the effects of gravity created by Earth's rotation and the pull of the Sun and Earth's Moon. In areas where high and low tide cause a big difference in sea levels, the movement of all this water can be used to generate electricity.

Tidal energy can be harnessed by using tidal streams, **barrages**, or tidal lagoons. All three methods use moving water to spin a turbine and power a generator. A tidal stream is a fast-moving ocean current produced by the tide. Turbines that look like underwater windmills are placed in a tidal stream. A barrage is a type of low dam, built across a river near to where it meets the sea. It has gates that are left open as the tide rises. Then they close, creating a tidal pool. When the water is released, it flows through the barrage's turbines to generate energy. The water is released at low tide, when water levels are most different, so there is greater potential energy in the trapped water.

A tidal lagoon is a body of ocean water that is partly enclosed. Lagoons can be used to generate electricity similar to barrages, by using water flowing from the lagoon to spin turbines. A tidal lagoon can be built along the coastline, and it can be made of rocks or other natural materials.

The Moon's gravity is strong enough to have an effect on the world's oceans.

Progress So Far

Tidal power is still being researched and developed. There are only a handful of working tidal power stations around the world, and most of them are quite small. More are in the planning stages. However, tidal power is suitable only for some locations. Russia, South Korea, and the United Kingdom are some of the countries looking into tidal power.

The Annapolis Royal Generating Station in Nova Scotia is the largest power station in North America to generate electricity from tides. The large tides of the Bay of Fundy help power this station.

FAST FORWARD

The first license for a commercial tidal power station in the United States was granted in 2012. The project involves installing up to 30 turbines in the East River in New York City. Installing the large turbines 33 feet (10 m) below a busy river will be a challenge, but developers hope that the project will eventually provide electricity for thousands of homes. Could this be the first of many new tidal energy projects? Why or why not?

Tidal Pros and Cons

Tidal energy has many of the same benefits as wave power and hydroelectric power. It is renewable and does not produce pollution or greenhouse gases. It does not need fuel to run, and the tides provide a predictable and consistent source of energy. Once the cost of building and installing the turbines is earned back, the energy is low-cost.

However, tidal energy also has its disadvantages. One of the main problems is that it can be used only in limited locations. In many places on Earth, the difference between high and low tides is fairly small. To be efficient, a tidal energy project needs to be located somewhere with a big range between high and low tides. In addition, these projects can generate power only when the tide is actually moving in or out. This is about 10 hours over the course of a 24-hour day.

So far, a lot of tidal energy technology is new and unproven. Researching and developing a new type of tidal energy set-up takes a lot of money, and there is no guarantee that it will ever make money. This makes governments and businesses less willing to invest in it.

Ocean Flow Energy.com

evo pod

The Evopod has a turbine that floats just below the water's surface. It is moored to the seabed.

Environmental Impact

Turbines in tidal streams have the potential to get in the way of ships and to disturb wildlife. However, they still have less of an environmental impact than a tidal barrage. These structures change the water level in the tidal pool, make the water less salty, and can cause a build-up of sand, soil, and mud (called **silt**) which sinks to the bottom of the pool. Plants and animals that live there may not be able to adjust to the changed conditions. The barrages block fish and other animals from moving in or out, and some can be caught in the turbines.

Wading birds, such as this oystercatcher, find food in the mudflats of tidal estuaries. Building barrages could affect their feeding grounds.

The Energy Future: You Choose

Tidal lagoons are a good alternative to building barrages. Their barriers can be designed to be submerged at high tide, so animals can swim over or around them. So far, none have been built, but a few are in the planning stages. Unfortunately, they will likely produce less energy than tidal barrages. What factors would you consider if you had to make a decision about building a tidal power project? Give reasons for your answers.

Power Up!

Harnessing the energy of moving water is a good way to power our lives. It is renewable and clean, and using it means burning less coal, oil, and natural gas. However, using clean energy is just part of the solution. We need to find ways to use less energy as well.

What Can You Do?

You can help by looking at your daily electricity usage. Are there areas where you could cut down? Instead of leaving them on standby, turn off gadgets and appliances when you are not using them. Cut down on heating and cooling by adding or removing layers of clothing instead of adjusting the thermostat. Using less electricity helps protect the planet and it will also save your family money.

You may not live in an area where hydroelectric power is available, but in some places, you can choose where your energy comes from. Do a little research and see if you can help your parents or caregivers find an energy provider that uses renewable sources instead of fossil fuels.

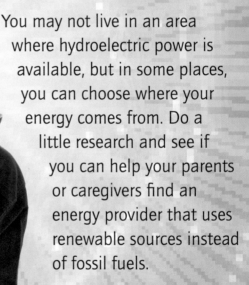

It may take more effort to find renewable sources of energy, but it is definitely worth it.

Activity:

Hydroelectric power depends on the movement of water to spin turbines. This activity shows you how to make a simple water turbine.

You Will Need:

- Cork
- Craft knife
- 2 clean, empty 67 oz (2 L) bottles
- Pen
- Pair of scissors
- Wooden barbecue skewer
- 2 paper clips
- Tape
- Wide-mouthed funnel
- An adult to help
- Running water

Instructions

1. Measure the length of the cork. Ask an adult to cut the top and bottom off a plastic bottle, leaving a cylinder that is as high as the cork is long.
2. Cut six equal-sized strips from the cylinder that are the same length as the cork but only half as wide as they are long.
3. Draw six evenly spaced lines on the cork. Ask an adult to cut a slit on each line with the craft knife.
4. Insert the pieces of bottle into the slits. They should all curve in the same direction.
5. Cut the skewer in half. Put each half into one end of a cork.
6. Unfold the paper clips and twist the top end of each one to make a loop. Tape the bottom ends to each side of the mouth of the funnel.
7. Stick the skewers through the paper clip loops so that the cork is over the funnel. Place the funnel in the mouth of the second bottle. Place your turbine under a tap.

cork

funnel

bottle

water

What Happened?

When running water hits your turbine, it should spin. Experiment by turning the tap to change how fast the water flows, and by moving the funnel so that it is closer or farther away from the tap. What do these changes do to the speed of the turbine?

Glossary

Please note: Some bold-faced words are defined where they appear in the text

barrages Artificial barriers built across a river or estuary to prevent flooding, help with irrigation, or generate electricity

buoys Floating objects moored to the bottom of a body of water

carbon dioxide A gas molecule made of a carbon atom joined with two oxygen atoms

chemical reactions Processes that change one or more substances into new substances

climate change Changes to the usual weather patterns in an area or to the entire Earth

commercial For business or profit

dam A wall built across a river or stream to keep the water from flowing

deltas Large areas of soil deposited at the mouth of some large rivers

droughts Long periods of time with lower than average rainfall

elevation Height above sea level

energy The ability to do work. Energy can take many different forms

engineers People whose job it is to use or design machines

fossil fuels Energy sources made from the remains of plants and animals that died millions of years ago and were buried

fuels Things, such as wood or gasoline, that can be burned as a source of energy

generators Machines that change movement into electrical energy

gravity The force that attracts all objects toward each other

green Not damaging to the environment

greenhouse gas A gas, such as carbon dioxide and methane, which contributes to the greenhouse effect

habitats Places where a plant or animal usually lives

hydroelectric Electric energy created by water power

intake The place at which water is taken into a hydroelectric installation

investment Money given to help develop a product or idea, in the hope that it will earn enough to pay back the money

kilowatts Units of measure for energy. There are 1,000 watts in a kilowatt

megawatts Units of measure for energy. There are 1 million watts in a megawatt

nuclear power The electricity generated by nuclear reactions

penstock A tube or other structure for carrying water to a waterwheel or turbine

pollution Something introduced into the environment that causes harmful or poisonous effects

renewable Something that renews itself once it is used

reservoir A lake-like body of water that forms behind a dam

silt Tiny pieces of sand, soil, and mud that are carried in water and eventually settle at the bottom

solar power Electricity generated by harnessing the energy of the Sun

sustainable A way of living that conserves and efficiently uses natural resources

tides The regular changes in the height of the surface of the oceans, caused by the pull of the Moon's gravity

turbines Machines in which a rotor is made to turn by the power of the wind, moving water, or steam

weir A small, low dam built in a river for the purpose of backing up or diverting water

Learning More

Find out more about electricity generated from water.

Books

Barker, Geoff. *How Renewable Energy Works* (ECO Works). Gareth Stevens Publishing, 2013.

Bjorklund, Ruth. *The Pros and Cons of Hydropower* (Economics of Energy). Cavendish Square Publishing, 2014.

Rusch, Elizabeth. *The Next Wave: The Quest to Harness the Power of the Oceans* (Scientists in the Field). HMH Books for Young Readers, 2014.

Websites

The United States Geological Survey provides information on hydroelectric power at:
http://water.usgs.gov/edu/hyhowworks.html

National Geographic has information about hydroelectricity and a photo gallery of major dams at:
http://education.nationalgeographic.co.uk/encyclopedia/hydroelectric-energy/

Visit the Environmental Protection Agency website for a list of pros and cons about hydroelectricity at:
www.epa.gov/cleanenergy/energy-and-you/affect/hydro.html

Index

Albania 12
Argentina 13

Brazil 12, 13

California 11
Canada 7, 12, 19
CETO technology 20
China 7, 12, 13, 15, 17
climate change 4, 17

dams 7, 8, 10–11, 12, 13, 14, 15, 16, 17, 18, 19, 24
droughts 11, 16

electricity 4, 5, 6, 7, 8, 9, 10, 11, 12, 13, 14, 15, 16, 18, 19, 20, 21, 22, 24, 25, 28
energy 4–5, 6, 7, 8–9, 10, 11, 14, 15, 16, 18, 19, 20, 21, 23, 24, 25, 26, 27, 28
England 6
Ethiopia 12

fossil fuels 8, 9, 12, 18, 19, 28
France 25

gravity 4, 11, 24
greenhouse gases 17, 19, 22, 26

Hawaii 20

India 13
Indonesia 15

Mozambique 12

Nepal 12
nonrenewable 9
Norway 12

Paraguay 12, 13
Pelamis 20, 21
pollution 4, 19, 22, 26
Portugal 21

renewable 8–9, 12, 18, 19, 22, 26, 28
run-of-the-river plants 11, 12, 15
Russia 12, 25

tides 7, 24, 26, 27

United States 7, 12, 13, 25

waves 4, 6, 7, 20–21, 22–23, 26
Wisconsin 6, 7